This book is dedicated to the men and women of the Graves Registration Service whose grim, discreet labor ensured the fitting burial of over 70,000 Americans in Europe.

NOBODY HAD SEEN THE LIKE. They had the smart uniforms, the chewing gum, the nylons, the Hershie bars and they called the ladies 'Ma'am'. Some of them were black. Some were 'Indian'. They seemed so tall, so fit, so courteous – and so well paid. These were the 'Yanks'.

Two million Americans had landed in France during 1917–18; now, in 1944–45, two million of them came again, pouring onto the beaches and into the ports of Normandy to batter their way towards Berlin.

But the currency of war is death, and by the end of the Second World War 31,744 Americans would be buried in Normandy and 141,305 in Europe – almost half the total of burials worldwide, and three times the First World War figure.

Without their sacrifice, Allied victory in either war, and the freedoms we today take for granted, would have been impossible.

The Purple Heart is awarded to all US personnel killed or wounded in action.

'It was the first time I shoot at living men. I don't remember exactly how it was; the only thing I know is that I went to my machine gun and I shoot, I shoot, I shoot.'
UNNAMED GERMAN PRIVATE ON THE BLUFFS AT WN62

THE CEMETERY OVERLOOKS 'EASY RED' SECTOR, the longest of the eight Omaha sectors. This was assaulted on D-Day June 6, 1944, by the 16th Infantry Regiment of the 1st Division on its third amphibious landing of the Second World War. (Old regulars joked that the US army consisted of the 1st Division and 8 million replacements!) Their memorial stands outside the cemetery overlooking the bluffs and beach.

The 1st Division had been the first of General Pershing's 'doughboys' (infantrymen) at the Western Front in 1917. The fighting conditions their successors would encounter in Normandy would be just as slow, dangerous and bloody; with the weight and accuracy of fire-power bearing down on them, things were arguably worse.

Also on Easy Red were inexperienced men of the 29th Division, supposed to have landed to the west. No one in either division could have conceived of the carnage to follow.

Robert Capa, the war photographer, once back on board ship after taking dramatic pictures of the landings at Easy Red, witnessed the continuing disembarkations: 'The last wave of the 16th Infantry were just being lowered, but the decks were already full with the return-ing wounded and the dead ... the mess boys who had served our coffee in white jackets and white gloves at three in the morning were covered in blood and were sewing the dead into white sacks.'

By the end of June 1944, 27,000 US casualties had been evacuated altogether, and 11,000 GIs had been killed in action or died of their wounds.

On Easy Red, men pinned down on the shingle. A man stands before withering fire on the right. 'Courage,' said Churchill, 'is the first of all human qualities, because it guarantees all others.'

The dead are sown into white sacks on a hospital ship, for burial in Cambridge, England.

June 7, Le Ruquet: troops of 2nd ID stream past WN65, a bunker still in place half a mile (1km) west of the cemetery.

Captain Thomas P. Moundres, 14:28, Company Commander of a mortar unit, 16th Infantry Regiment, before landing held a meeting with all his company's officers, wished them good luck and said goodbye. Perhaps he had a premonition of impending death. He was killed by a mortar shell just as he reached land.

SUGGESTED WEBSITES

www.britannica.com/normandy/week
www.ddaymuseum.org
www.bigredone.org

'There are few things worse than being a rifleman in the infantry, but being a medic is one of them. When the shelling and shooting is heavy, the regular GIs can press themselves into their holes and don't need to go out on a mission of mercy.'
BRIAN WHITMARSH, A MEDIC OF 99TH DIVISION

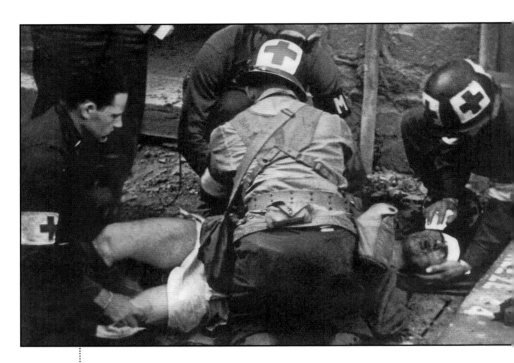

Mostly enlisted men with only basic training, medics were called upon to perform miracles of 'foxhole' surgery. In some campaigns proportionately more US medics were killed than fighting troops. Over 3,000 of them were killed in the Second World War.

COMBAT MEDICS LANDED IN THE INITIAL ASSAULT, but at Omaha were limited by continuous fire and shortage of equipment to administering plasma and treating the wounded for shock. Attempts to assemble the wounded for evacuation only attracted deadly accurate mortar rounds, and many lying helpless and exposed on the sand were hit a second or third time by rifle and machine gun fire.

An army surgeon with the 16th Infantry Regiment, Major Charles Tegtmeyer, at 08.15 hrs on D-Day morning, recalled, 'Face downward, as far as the eyes could see in either direction, were the huddled bodies of men living, wounded and dead, packed together like cigars in a pack. Everywhere the frantic cry, "Medic ... hey, Medic!" could be heard above the horrible din.' A Navy doctor working in 'pink, murky water ... could not distinguish the living from the dead'.

Too often soldiers had replaced personal medical kit with cigarettes and candy, but later, incoming landing craft brought further medical supplies and a first aid station was established up the beach. At sea, countless men survived through the seamanship of Coast Guard crews. However, not all the wounded could be retrieved. The night of D-Day was pierced by the nerve-wracking screams of broken men isolated by minefields.

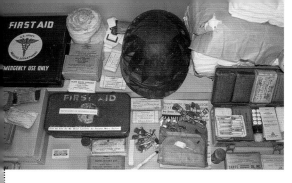

Dropped well behind enemy lines, the para-
trooper carried a simple first-aid kit of bandages,
sulfa drugs and morphine, shown here at the
Airborne Museum, Sainte-Merè-Eglise.

SUGGESTED WEBSITES

www.ww2medicine.org
Listen to men and women at Omaha at:
www.nationalgeographic.com/ngm/0206

But despite the horrors of battle, men had a far higher
chance of surviving than in the First World War, owing to
improvements in medicine and surgery: the introduction of
blood banks, anti-bacterial sulfa powder and, above all, antibi-
otics such as penicillin. A wounded German's best chance of
surviving was to be cared for by Allied medics. From medic to
aid station, to field or evacuation hospital, the wounded soldier
had an 85 per cent chance of recovery, an extraordinary tribute
to the work of field nurses, surgeons and doctors.

On June 10, ten days ahead of schedule, a landing strip
became operational on high ground one mile (1½km) west
of the present cemetery. The air evacuation of casualties
could begin. Almost all survived the sea journey, but evacuation
by air was even safer. Worldwide, only 46 of over one million
died en route.

To veteran riflemen the only
escape was the stretcher or the
grave. The million-dollar wound
was the one that got you back
home with no disfigurement
and minimum pain.

Men of the 6th Naval Beach Battalion awaiting evacuation. John Gallagher, bandaged on
the far right, had been given up for dead, but
his body today — very much alive — carries
so much shrapnel that he says, 'I try to
stay away from magnets'.

> '*If every civilian in the world could smell this stink, then maybe we wouldn't have any more wars.*'
>
> TECHNICAL SERGEANT HAGUALL, GRAVES REGISTRATION UNIT

AT 19.30 HRS 70 MEN AND THREE OFFICERS of the 453rd Medical Collecting Company landed with the gruesome assignment of collecting up the remaining wounded, bodies and human remains from the beach. The morning after D-Day, June 7, as control was established over the fragile beachhead, the traffic along the shoreline was such that both the living and the dead risked being run over. For ten days, corpses were washed in with the tide, and it was nothing for a man to walk along the beach and see disembodied arms, legs or fingers. For those who had never seen or touched a dead body before it was a hard induction to war.

Originally, two sites for the first cemeteries in Omaha sector were planned, but these were 5 miles (8km) inland, deep in enemy-held territory. The Germans were still firing on the beach and most beach exits remained blocked. Priority had to be given to getting the living and their supplies inland. But at 08.35 hrs, after checking for mines, a bulldozer was used to dig trenches for a temporary cemetery on the level, open, sandy ground at Dog Red. Hundreds of POWs (prisoners of war) were put to work, helped by the black Quartermaster Companies and others.

Bodies were wrapped in cotton mattress covers, and each grave was marked with a short white stake with the dead man's dog tag draped over the top (see page 8). By midnight on June 10/11, 457 Americans and some German, Royal Navy and RAF dead were buried in what was also known as 'V Corps Cemetery'. But the smell and the flies were bad.

With further ground gained and troops pouring along the beach road – widened to serve the new Mulberry Harbor – a service was held on the Sunday. Then, for the sake of both morale and hygiene, the bodies were transferred over the next ten days to the No.2 burial ground being created behind the bluff east of Le Ruquet valley.

By June 26, 1,510 Americans, 48 British and 606 Germans were buried or reburied there. The final tally of American burials was 3,808. This site of 'Provisional Cemetery No.2' eventually determined the position of America's permanent cemetery in Normandy.

The booted, sheeted dead lying in the damp sand. In the background are black Quartermaster Companies with the requisitioned bulldozer. In 2003 Wilmott Ragsdale, aged 92, revisited the spot where he had taken this picture as a war correspondent on June 9, 1944.

While still under constant sniper fire, and artillery fire from inland, all through June 7 the bodies were collected up and laid out for identification on the flat ground between the road and the bluff. Their equipment was stacked for re-use.

Major Thomas Howie (G14:12), the 'Major of Saint-Lô', was killed by shrapnel on July 17, 1944 while leading an attack on the town. After the battle, his body was ceremoniously taken into the shattered town on a jeep and laid before the ruins of Sainte-Croix church, his body draped in the Stars and Stripes. However, the press reported that Howie was killed by a sniper and had been carried into Saint-Lô on the shoulders of his men in fulfillment of his last wish.

No one can ever know precisely how many died on D-Day itself. A rough Allied figure is some 2,900 military and 2,000 civilian deaths – a quarter of the expected toll. But a grim 77-day 'killing match' followed in the Normandy countryside.

SUGGESTED WEBSITES

Useful D-Day links at:
www.historyguy.com/normandy_links.html
www.normandyallies.org/1hist.htm
www.historyoftheworld.com/sequel/ww2.htm

German prisoners of war, housed near Le Ruquet, digging at the Saint Laurent No.2 cemetery. Note the forest of crosses in the background, each leaning against the stake it will replace.

'We learned quickly how to handle remains with reverence.'
SERGEANT CHARLES D. BUTTE, 3RD PLATOON, ATTACHED TO THE 90TH DIVISION, 603RD QUARTERMASTER COY

THE FIRST BURIALS AND IDENTIFICATION OF AMERICANS in France were carried out by French civilians and the German authorities: these concerned air crew who had taken part in operations over France from 1942. If the crash site was located and the men identified, the International Red Cross was informed. Nearly all the reinterments in the Normandy Cemetery dating from before D-Day are airmen.

Proper identification by the Grave Registration Service was a priority. Two dog tags, worn at all times, bore name, service number and, until March 1944, next of kin, religion and blood group. One tag was left with the body and the other passed forward for notification. Pay books, vaccination cards, letters from home, even laundry marks, along with other personal possessions, were carefully logged and photographed. Fingerprints, birthmarks and other physical characteristics also provided vital clues.

Quartermaster Sergeant Elbert E. Legg was flown in on D-Day with the task of marking out, alone, the first cemetery in Utah (VII Corps) sector, at Blosville south of Sainte-Mère-Eglise. For the first few days local civilians dug the graves.

Such was the intensity of the hedgerow fighting inland that three more US temporary cemeteries were soon established within 6 miles (10km) of Utah Beach.

Dog tags. The notch was for fitting to the embossing machine, not into teeth as was rumored.

Graves Registration units arrived on June 9, by which time hundreds of bodies, about half of them German, were awaiting identification and burial. While casualties on Utah Beach had been light, the killing among the airborne troops alone – over 1,000 eventually – was as brutally high as on Omaha Beach. Scattered over a wide area, in crashed and burnt gliders, burnt-out vehicles, hanging

A Graves Registration Officer notes down the identification details of bodies recently recovered from the battlefield. The painstaking work of identification began in November 1945 and was largely over by July 1949.

After Joe Beyrle (101st Airborne) was taken POW on D-Day, a German spy took his dog tags and uniform to infiltrate Allied lines. However, the spy was killed (probably by Germans) and Beyrle's parents received a KIA (killed in action) telegram. It was only in early 1945 that Beyrle was liberated by Russian troops and his survival confirmed. After fighting in the Soviet army he was thus able to visit his own grave!

THIS MARKS THE SITE OF FIRST AMERICAN CEMETERY IN FRANCE WORLD WAR II SINCE MOVED TO AMERICAN CEMETERY N° I

Emplacement du 1er cimetière américain
Débarquement de Juin 1944

1st	Infantry Division
29th	Infantry Division
5th	Engineer Special Brigade
6th	Engineer Special Brigade

The No.1 marker can be found on the beach road at 'Dog White', between Saint Laurent and Vierville.

from trees or drowned in the flooded marshes, the bodies were harder to recover. The first cemetery at Sainte-Mère-Eglise quickly filled, so a second site to the south was opened on June 25. On June 20, a cemetery at Orglandes 5 miles (8km) west was created for Americans, but most of the dead brought in were German. Again, hundreds of POWs were put to work digging graves, while the French handled and moved the bodies, and maintained the sites. Many airborne troops were shrouded in their own parachute silks. Blosville had swollen to 5,700 by July 1.

American graves were first marked by white stakes, later by white stencilled wooden crosses and a few Stars of David; Germans with smaller, black crosses. All the commanders made frequent visits. General Collins of VII Corps tried to ensure that all the American bodies were buried the day they arrived, whatever the difficulties. Identification caused the longest delay. German bodies were at first allowed to stack, but eventually received the same treatment. In the three burial grounds outside Sainte-Mère-Eglise, 12,708 US graves were eventually dug.

By April 1945, 76,360 Americans were buried in the 24 temporary cemeteries on and in French soil. Plans laid down in 1947 for a permanent cemetery at Blosville were never realized.

SUGGESTED WEBSITES

www.qmfound.com/mortuary-affairs.htm
www.airborne.museum.org

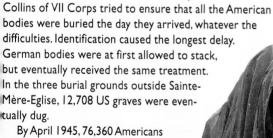

Disinterred bodies were brought to the laboratory for identification and analysis in temporary wooden caskets marked 'head' and 'foot'.

'Some of the men buried here were my personal friends. All of them, whether they believed in Christ, Jehovah or Allah, regardless of their creed, all of them are in the hands of a Supreme Being.'
SPEECH BY GENERAL GERHARDT AT LA CAMBE, JULY 23, 1944

The 1st, 7th and 9th Armies segregated the dead as seen here; Patton's 3rd Army established separate cemeteries for US and German burials, which made arrangements easier after the war.

ON SATURDAY JUNE 10, another site, at La Cambe, 5 miles (8km) inland from Omaha Beach, began to receive American and German dead (in separate plots) from the hedgerow fighting. Six weeks later, in a touching ceremony, with many unburied dead piled up on either side of the honor guard, it was dedicated by General Gerhardt to his 29th Division, the 'Blues and Grays'. By then, nearly all the 29th's 5,000 riflemen were casualties and had been replaced – '29ers' said that an old soldier was one who had survived three days in the line. The names of over 2,000 Americans who lay at La Cambe were read out – the total would eventually reach 4,534. Today 911 '29ers' are buried or memorialized in the Normandy American cemetery.

The killing went on: within a week, three more temporary burial grounds had been created, at Marigny (July 31; 3,070), at Saint James (August 5; 4,367) and at Le Chêne Guérin (August 7; 1,202).

The impact of a soldier's death fell on families back in the US about a month later. In towns big and small across America, ticker-tape machines in telegraph offices would clatter out the dry official notification: 'The Secretary of War desires me to express his deep sympathy that your husband/son ... was killed in action on [date] in France. Letter follows'. The narrow tape was glued onto a telegram form for some unfortunate messenger to deliver.

A remarkable piece of ephemera in the Airborne Museum: the cardboard stencil used to mark the name on the temporary grave of William Loudermilk.

WM A LOUDERMILK
34198753

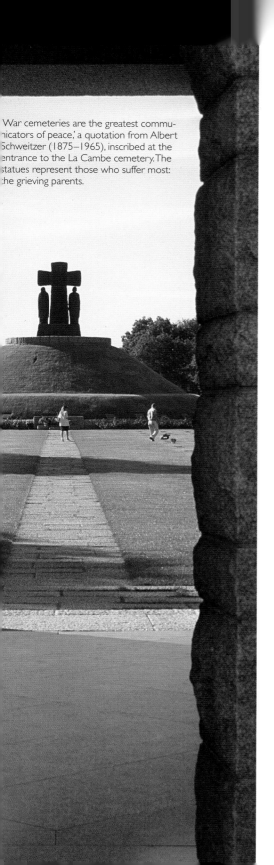

'War cemeteries are the greatest commu-
nicators of peace,' a quotation from Albert
Schweitzer (1875–1965), inscribed at the
entrance to the La Cambe cemetery. The
statues represent those who suffer most:
the grieving parents.

Lieutenant Ollie Reed died in the Italian campaign
in early July, and his father, Colonel Ollie Reed of
the 29th Division, was shot in his jeep near Saint-
Lô on July 30. The two telegrams arrived at the
family home within 45 minutes of each other.
(E20:19,20)

One of the most painful tasks for a commanding officer
and the chaplain to perform was to write to the families of
men who had died. Most wives and parents bore the news
with stoic resignation. The enormity of what was happening
in Normandy came across in the terse phrases of newspaper
announcements: 'missing presumed killed'; 'died of wounds';
'killed in action, aged 21'.

'In pious homage to our liberating friends.' On the
French National Day, July 14, Saint-Lô and part of
Caen were still in enemy hands.

SUGGESTED WEBSITES

www.29thdivision.com
www.staunton.com/116th

> *'I think the first telegram was a surprise, but they kept coming; the feelings turned to shock and then an overwhelming sadness.'*
> ELIZABETH TEASS, TELEGRAPH OPERATOR IN BEDFORD, VIRGINIA

ON ONE DAY – SUNDAY JULY 16 – in Bedford (population 3,000), Elizabeth Teass watched 19 messages from Europe come through. In all, over half the men conscripted from Bedford County would be killed. The sheriff, the drugstore delivery clerk, the taxi driver and the funeral director delivered the telegrams.

From the sheriff, John and Macey Hoback learned that their elder son Bedford (30) had been killed. One of Bedford's sisters, Lucille Boggess, recalls, 'On Monday, my sister and I tried to cheer up our folks by making ice cream. We were in the basement when the second telegram came.' Her other brother, Raymond (24), was missing in action. Both brothers had died on Omaha Beach, Raymond overwhelmed in the rising tide and lost to the sea.

As news of the tragedy spread, the initial shock turned to overpowering grief. The church service was cancelled and the entire congregation came to the Hoback house. The effect on such a small community was devastating.

A few weeks later a small parcel arrived containing Raymond's Bible; mortally wounded, he had evidently managed to push it, in its waterproof bag, up out of the reach of the tide. The suffering of Bedford County symbolized the solidarity and grief of the whole nation, and led to the creation of the D-Day Memorial there, where survivors work tirelessly to teach the young about the sacrifice of their generation.

Bedford Hoback (right; G10:28) and his brother Raymond (Wall of the Missing) were infantrymen. Raymond suffered from chronic nosebleeds and could have stayed home. In the group photo, Bedford is in the foreground with his fiancée, Elaine Coffey, before he headed for England.

On June 9, 1944, Mrs Niland received a 'missing in action' telegram: her eldest son, Eddy (31), had been shot down over Burma on May 16. On June 19, she received two telegrams within half an hour of each other, saying that her son, Robert (25; 82nd Airborne), had been killed on D-Day, and that another son, Preston (29; 4th Division), had been killed the day after. Her youngest son, Fritz (24, 101st Airborne), was fighting near Carentan. Father Simpson, the divisional chaplain, wanted him to demobilize and return to New York to be with his mother but, according to Fritz's daughter, he finished his tour of duty in Normandy until relieved on July 8. Both Fritz and Eddy survived the war. This story inspired the fictional narrative for the movie *Saving Private Ryan*.

'Please, don't worry mother, everything will be fine. Wait, pray and hope; don't worry, all the guys will come back safe and sound, this war will soon be over. One evening we will soon all be back together and it will all seem like a long dream.'
PRESTON NILAND

Robert and Preston Niland lie at F15:11,12; there are 38 pairs of brothers, 33 of whom lie together. Graves were allocated at random except for family, some air crews and, as a result of last requests, friends.

Four women are buried in the cemetery: three from the Women's Army Corps killed in a vehicle crash, and Elizabeth Richardson, an American Red Cross nurse who died in an air accident, all in July 1945. (D20:46; A19:30; F13:19; A21:5)

Roy and Ray Stevens of Bedford were both in the first wave on Omaha Beach, but in different landing craft. Ever since, Roy has asked himself, 'Why him and not me?'

SUGGESTED WEBSITES

www.private-ryan.eb.com
www.dday.org

Here a family visits one of the 149 Jewish graves: Jews were advised to 'lose' their dog tags before capture (the embossed H indicated Hebrew). Pfc. Hyman and Staff Sgt. Martin Goland, two Jewish brothers, lie together (J8: 24, 25) and were killed within eight days of each other.

*'It is foolish and wrong to mourn the men who died.
Rather we should thank God that such men lived.'*
GENERAL GEORGE C. PATTON JUNE 7, 1945

Close-typed lists of US war casualties from the Library of Congress form a silent but eloquent barometer of American determination, as expressed by President Roosevelt, 'to win through to absolute victory no matter how long it may take'.

MOST US NEXT OF KIN (61 per cent) opted for repatriation, a choice not in the tradition of any other nation. The sheer number of finished caskets required in this process led to a delay; disinterment from the temporary cemetery at Saint Laurent only began on September 16, 1947, two days after a benediction ceremony attended by thousands of French families, veterans and many dignitaries. By the end of October, all 3,808 bodies had been removed.

Bodies either went in the temporary wooden caskets to a canvas mausoleum outside Saint Laurent, or were placed in metal 'repatriation' caskets and stored in a Cherbourg warehouse for shipment, each draped in the US flag.

A week later, on November 4, 1947, the *Robert F. Burns* left port with 1,052 caskets, picking up 4,200 more in Antwerp, the other port in Europe used for this purpose. From the quayside at Brooklyn army base in New York, the caskets were then taken to one of 15 centers across the nation, and on by local train or carrier to the families. Mortuary trains had as many as 15 carriages, each holding up to 66 caskets. Every stage of the long journey home was marked by ceremonies, and a military escort was provided by the government for each body in its flag-draped casket.

The process was largely over by 1951, by which time 17,949 bodies had been shipped out of Cherbourg. Worldwide, 233,181 bodies were eventually returned to the US in this way.

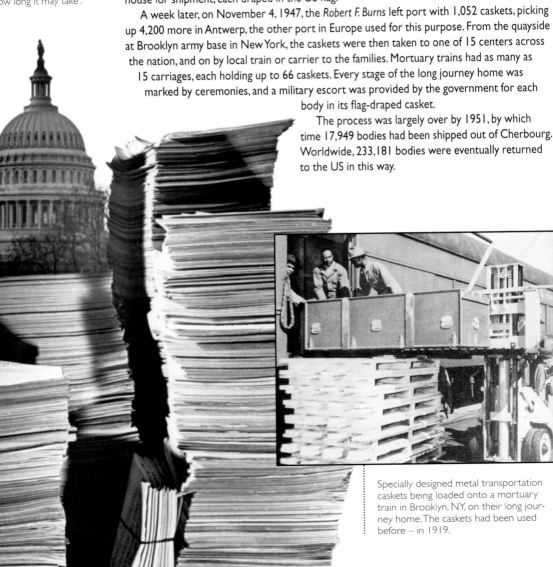

Specially designed metal transportation caskets being loaded onto a mortuary train in Brooklyn, NY, on their long journey home. The caskets had been used before – in 1919.

Flag-draped transportation caskets in a Cherbourg warehouse await repatriation to the US. Similar facilities were used at Antwerp, Belgium, for the later campaigns.

The 1st Division memorial recalls John J. Pinder, 16th Infantry, who received a posthumous Medal of Honor in January 1945 for conspicuous bravery after battling forward on Easy Red (see page 2), badly wounded and under heavy fire, to deliver his radio. In terrible pain and refusing medical assistance he went back three times into the surf to salvage vital communication equipment until he was killed after successfully setting it up. He was reburied in Burgettstown, Pennsylvania, in May 1948.

Through November 1947 La Cambe was cleared, eventually becoming the largest Second World War cemetery in Normandy – or Germans (21,555). Orglandes holds 10,152 Germans today. The contrasting architecture and Teutonic mood makes both places well worth a visit, as is the exhibition at La Cambe on the German cemeteries and the commitment of young people in Europe to maintaining them.

The American Battle Monument Commission was established in 1923. At first under Generals John J. Pershing (1923–48) and George C. Marshall (1948–59), the ABMC looks after 24 overseas cemeteries, of which two are in Normandy: the Brittany American Cemetery near Mont Saint Michel, is in fact in Normandy! They are financed by American taxes.

American and French children come to pay their respects and to learn. Where once the American dead were repatriated from all over the world, now the living come from all over the world to those Americans who remain 'in perpetuity' in France.

SUGGESTED WEBSITES

www.americanwardead.com
Search on 'Burual'* and 'Deceased Information'
*At the time of going to press, 'Burual' works, but the correct spelling does not.

> *'It is to them that we and all future generations must pay grateful tribute.'*
> PRESIDENT FRANKLIN D. ROOSEVELT

THE 172-ACRE (72-HA) CEMETERY SITE at Colleville-Saint-Laurent was given by France to the United States in perpetuity, free of tax, with the status of US territory. The burial ground itself is the second largest in number in France, after the Lorraine cemetery (10,489).

Immediately west of the cemetery lies Le Ruquet valley, site of WN65. Beyond, the Saint Laurent airstrip once took up the open ground. Beyond again, the whole arc of Omaha Beach comes into view.

The first grave was dug on November 4, 1948 to receive a body in its permanent metal casket. Concrete beams straddle the site to ensure the perfect alignment of the crosses, and the characteristic 'bellying' of the layout. The headstones are of white Italian 'Lasa' marble, 149 being Jewish Stars of David and 307 being unknowns, bearing the inscription 'A Comrade in Arms Known but to God'.

On December 28, 1949, with 9,350 interments complete, work could begin on the architectural elements, designed by Harbeson, Livingston and Larson of Philadelphia, using Vaurion limestone for the loggias, colonnade and chapel. The non-denominational chapel lies at the heart of a ground plan of paths that form a Latin cross. Inside, a remarkable mosaic ceiling represents America blessing her sons as they set out by sea and air, a grateful France honoring the dead, and the return of peace symbolized by an angel, dove and homeward-bound ship.

West of the chapel, the cemetery extends to an opening in the trees, framed by two Italian granite statues. One bears the eagle of the USA, the other the cockerel of France. Beyond, across the former airfield, the rebuilt steeple of Vierville Church can be seen, the surrounding land being protected by strict planning laws.

'If I stood there on the beach I would not just see white crosses, I would see the fathers and brothers and the sweethearts under those crosses, and I don't ever want to see that reminder again.' Flight Nurse Evelyn Kowalchuk has never returned to Normandy or the site of the airfield at Le Ruquet where she flew in and out evacuating the wounded.

Most visitors head for Roosevelt (D28:46; see page 20) but there are graves of two other generals, Lt. Gen. Lesley McNair (F28:42), Brig. Gen. Nelson Walker (B23:47) and two other 'Medals of Honor' (see page 21 and map).

Cypress trees, shrubs and roses punctuate the formality of the gravestone areas. On July 18, 1956, 14 years to the day after the opening of the first US temporary cemetery in Europe (at Brookwood, England), the Normandy American Cemetery was inaugurated. The following day, the Brittany American Cemetery at Saint James (4,410 graves) was also formally opened. Only two interments have taken place in the Normandy cemetery since.

First Lt. Jimmy Monteith MOH, 1st ID, ignoring warnings for his own safety, led his assault group over the beach at Easy Red, went back to guide two tanks safely through a minefield and direct their fire, then led a successful attack until killed.

SUGGESTED WEBSITES

www.wwIImemorial.com
www.normandylandingbeaches.com
www.battlefieldsww2.50megs.com

The final tally of Americans 'missing in action' from the Battle of Normandy was much lower than North Africa or the Far East. Inscribed in alphabetical order and by order of service on the curved wall around the garden are 1,557 names, men killed in the violent outfall of explosions, men drowned or buried at sea, or men who crashed in their aircraft in bombing operations over France.

Of the names, 489 recall those lost with the USS Leopoldville, America's worst ship disaster of the war in the European theater.

Undelivered Christmas packages pile up in New York General Post Office marked 'Return to Sender – Killed in Action' (or Missing in Action).

The approach to the Garden of the Missing, by the statue entitled *American Youth Rising from the Waves*, the work of Donald de Lue of Leonardo, New Jersey.

The troopship USS *Leopoldville* lies 200 feet (60 metres) down and six miles (10km) off the French coast, the hole from the torpedo which sank it plain for any diver to see. It is, in effect, another of Normandy's war cemeteries, being the last resting place of many hundreds of American infantrymen.

THE TROOPSHIP USS *LEOPOLDVILLE* was a converted Belgian passenger ship, crewed by Belgians and Congolese. On Christmas Eve 1944, carrying 2,235 men of the 262nd and 264th Infantry Regiments of the 66th Division, it sailed from Southampton for Cherbourg, its 23rd such voyage.

At 17.54 hrs, six miles (10km) off the French coast, it was torpedoed. Over 300 men of the 262nd – at dinner – were killed outright, but the ship did not sink. It stood dead in the water awaiting a tow, the men forming in good order on the decks. An hour later the boilers exploded. As the *Leopoldville* began to list, most of the crew escaped, taking half the lifeboats. With no previous boat drill, the remaining boats were useless and the men had to jump, one by one, across the heaving, freezing sea onto the deck of a British escort destroyer.

At 20.30 hrs, 'Titanic' fashion, the bow lifted skywards with men still clinging on, then plunged to the seabed. Over 800 men died. Families received the standard 'killed in action' telegram, not knowing the truth until 1989 when the events were officially acknowledged and commemorations held. The 78 marked graves in the cemetery are dated December 25, 1944.

A CHRISTMAS TRAGEDY
'Forgotten by many, remembered by few.'
Clive Cussler, survivor

SUGGESTED WEBSITES

Find out more about the USS *Leopoldville* at:
www.members.aol.com/troopship/leopoldv.htm
www.history.navy.mil

France honors the American dead alongside the United States. President Réné Coty in 1956 said, 'They died for that France whose sons had, in former times, also crossed the Atlantic to answer the call of American Independence.'

Wall of the Missing (WOM). An asterisk identifies those who were subsequently recovered or identified. Each panel of names is separated by laurel leaves in low relief.

'When all is said and done, the most precious asset any nation has is its youth.'
GENERAL MATTHEW RIDGWAY, 'LEADERSHIP', *MILITARY REVIEW,* OCTOBER 1966

WITH OVER A MILLION VISITORS A YEAR, the Normandy American Cemetery is bursting with life. One of the traditional roles of the American Superintendent and his staff has been to inform and assist next of kin. But with the passage of time, films, educational programs and easier travel have served to heighten awareness and interest and put the cemetery at the heart of the Battle of Normandy story. The staff have a demanding commemorative, educational and diplomatic role to perform. Visits by heads of state and VIPs also require careful planning and strict security measures.

The cemetery's groundsmen work to maintain the immaculate lawns of Kentucky bluegrass as well as managing the plantations and sites at WN62, the Pointe du Hoc and Utah Beach for which the American Battle Monuments Commission is also responsible.

Memorial Day, the last Monday in May, is their 'longest day', when they take five hours to plant 19,674 French and American flags – two per grave.

In 1995 the 9,387th and final reburial, that of Sgt. Gafford Sanders (D25:46) took place, to join his brother, Sam (D7:7). The worldwide roll-call of the Second World War for US personnel amounted to 405,399 killed, of whom 78,976 would be unaccounted for.

Brigadier General Theodore Roosevelt Jnr., eldest son of the 26th President of the same name, badgered the authorities to let him land with the first wave of the 4th Division, feeling it would steady his troops 'to know I am with them'. At 56 and in frail health he landed at H-Hour on Utah Beach. In his wool-knit hat, he walked up and down Utah, flicking sand from shellbursts off his uniform, urging his men forward. His example and leadership led to the award of a Medal of Honor, but he did not live to hear either of this or his promotion to full General, for he suffered a fatal heart attack on July 12, 1944. Buried in Sainte-Mère-Eglise Provisional Cemetery No. 2, he was reburied in the Normandy American Cemetery in March 1948. Subsequently, the family requested that his brother Quentin, an aviator killed aged 21 in a dogfight near Reims in 1918, be reburied alongside him.